from Nicholas Roden
July 1987.

ROWLAND HILDER'S
ENGLAND

'The Dawn Leads on Another Day': a drawing for the frontispiece of *The Bible for Today*, published in 1941.

ROWLAND HILDER'S
ENGLAND

A personal record by the artist
introduced by Denis Thomas

THE HERBERT PRESS

First published in Great Britain by
The Herbert Press Limited, 46 Northchurch Road, London N1 4EJ
Reprinted twice in 1986

Designed by Pauline Harrison
Colour photography by Rado Klose
Colour separations by Royle Print
Typeset by Jolly & Barber Ltd, Rugby
Printed and bound in Hong Kong by South China Printing Co.

British Library Cataloguing in Publication Data

Hilder, Rowland
    Rowland Hilder's England.
    1. Hilder, Rowland
    I. Title
    759.2   ND1942.H5/

    ISBN 0-906969-57-3

Shell UK Ltd are pleased to sponsor this book in acknowledgement
of Rowland Hilder's long association with them.

Contents

Foreword

Many readers may recognise in these pages some paintings that have come their way in a different guise, as colour plates in publications issued by the old-established printing firm of Royles, with whom I have worked closely for over thirty years. In helping to bring them together in book form I have had the pleasure of re-living the occasions on which I sat down, with pencils, paints and brushes, to try to catch the mood and essence of each particular subject, on street corners, village greens, harbour walls, or a gently rocking boat.

In some cases, the scene has changed since then – probably not for the better from a painter's point of view. In others I have exercised the artist's right to select from the number of images at his disposal the ones that seem to express the essential spirit of the place. Often, as in the Shoreham Valley, familiar subjects present themselves in novel ways, no matter how many times I have painted them over the years.

No doubt every reader will have particular favourites, places known personally, to which are attached private thoughts and memories. Some may even have got out a tin of watercolours and set down their impressions – an activity which I have spent much of my life recommending to others, as well as practising myself. Whatever the response, it gives me renewed pleasure to think that 'Rowland Hilder's England' is by no means mine alone. It belongs to the thousands who share my love for it, and whose imaginations have been enriched by its plenty. Peter De Wint, one of the immortals among early English watercolour painters, once said that he had a 'beautiful profession'. So he had; and I am thankful to agree with him.

ROWLAND HILDER

Introduction

In northern Kent a long chalk ridge reaches across the county, broken by three rivers: in the east, the Kentish Stour; in the centre, the Medway; and in the west, the gentle Darent. Rowland Hilder knows them all, and has found some of his most characteristic subjects there. In particular, the stretch from Eynsford along the Shoreham Valley to Underriver, just north of Sevenoaks, seems to contain the essence of mood and place that one associates with his happiest work. The beech woods on the flanks of the valley, the farms and hopfields that he paints at all seasons, have inspired countless paintings and watercolours of the kind that his public recognise, at a glance, as 'Hilderscapes'.

The valley of the Darent has been a habitation since the Stone Age. Tools and shards have been found along its banks, notably at Lullingstone and Shoreham. Three thousand years separate its first residents from the cottagers and commuters of our own time. But the presence which haunts the valley is that of the Roman Britons, who were drawn there by its temperate weather and life-supporting environment. Stronger still, for Rowland Hilder, is the spirit of Samuel Palmer, a painter close to his heart, for whom, 150 years ago, this idyllic site became a 'Valley of Vision'.

Though Palmer spent less than twelve years there, they were the years in which he reached the height of his achievement as a painter, inspired by the rounded hills and sheltered fields of an enchanted landscape. It was as if, in this unknown English village, amid surroundings that seemed heaven-blessed, he entered a world already invented in his imagination. The valley, in Palmer's eyes, was an earthly paradise, divinely bounteous, ripened with heavenly love.

Rowland Hilder does not pretend to walk in Palmer's footsteps. But much of the 'Valley of Vision' is still there, to be painted. The Water House, by the little bridge, where Palmer lived with a small band of friends – the self-styled 'Ancients' – survives. So does Sepham Farm, with its hopfields; though not, regrettably, the great thatched barn that Palmer painted and drew. Hilder made his own record of it nearly forty years ago, before it was pulled down to make way for a modern version in corrugated iron. The original Sepham Barn does still appear from time to time, reincarnated in his paintings of the valley, since it exists vividly in Hilder's memory. The farm fields, trees, fences and tracks, and those of its neighbour, Filston Farm, figure in many a Hilder landscape, more often than not re-grouped in a synthesis of the scene rather than in literal terms. This is an attitude to the painter's task that Palmer would have approved. 'Nature is not at all the standard of art,' he wrote from Shoreham in 1825, 'but art is the standard of nature.'

While deeply attached to his favourite county, Rowland Hilder is not sure if he is a Man of Kent or a Kentish Man. Strictly speaking, trying to remember which side of the Medway is which, he thinks he may be neither: traditionally, a Man of Kent is one who comes from the east or south of the Medway, while a Kentish

Three illustrations, below and opposite, for a new edition of Mary Webb's *Precious Bane*, which included Rowland Hilder's first studies of the English landscape in winter.

Man hails from north or west of the river. For an artist so widely identified with the Garden of England it may seem surprising that he was born at Great Neck, Long Island. However, any American claims on him are ill-founded: he came to England in 1915, as a boy of ten, when his staunchly English father decided to return home and enlist in the army. The Hilder family embarked on the 'Lusitania' for the last voyage she was destined to make before being sunk by a German submarine. When the war was over, the Hilders settled down in their native land, this time for good.

It is hard, now, to think of Rowland Hilder in any other environment. His forbears were rooted in Kent, and he bears an old Kentish name. The tones and moods of his paintings are those of the southern English landscape: they emerge, almost of their own volition, in the very act of painting. In particular he responds to the countryside in its gaunt and bony season, before summer has clothed the naked trees and filled the bare fields with fruit and crops. He has remarked on how few of the early English landscape painters recorded the English scene in this guise; though he allows that sullen winter light and waterlogged roads must have had something to do with it. He first realised the potential of the winter landscape as a subject for a painter when, in 1928, he was approached by Jonathan Cape to illustrate a reissue of *Precious Bane*, one of the series of rural novels by Mary Webb, highly popular at the time, set in the villages and countryside of Shropshire. The Prime Minister of the day, Stanley Baldwin, contributed an introduction in which he remarked admiringly: 'Almost any page at random will furnish an illustration of the blending of human passion with the fields and skies.' It was the young Hilder's task to match these literary images with an artist's eye.

Mary Webb's genre of rustic story-telling is long out of fashion. But the chance it offered to create something original of his own was the first step towards Rowland Hilder's fulfilment as an artist. He hurried off to Shropshire, taking his future wife, Edith, with him. They stayed in the novelist's cottage at Lyth Hill, the better to soak in the atmosphere, from the beginning of November to the week before Christmas, looked after by Rowland's mother. If it was authenticity he was after, it was there in abundance: uncomfortably so, given the lingering unease of Mary Webb's ghost and the inevitably bitter weather.

The drawings for *Precious Bane* are the first 'Hilderscapes' (a term he dislikes, but has become resigned to). The winter trees, their shapes outlined in an aureole of twigs, and the bare fields scored by the plough, still retain their grace and freshness. Some thirty years later, Edith Hilder, herself a consummate flower painter, was to join Rowland in the month-by-month advertisements published as the *Shell Guide to Flowers of the Countryside*, with a text by Geoffrey Grigson, in which her lovingly drawn and botanically accurate watercolours were given landscape backgrounds in her husband's by then familiar style, including descendants of these prototype Hilder trees. (The twelve paintings, in series, had an estimated exposure of some 10 million a month.)

The sketches on which the Mary Webb illustrations were based are a vivid record of the young Hilder's excitement at seeing the countryside in an unexpectedly new light. In his sketchbooks, too, are studies of farm machinery, the interior of a wheelwright's shed, wagon wheels – new subjects to prompt the artist's curiosity, which he set down with his unerring pencil. He seized on the line 'Gideon and the oxen came on slow, making a little solid dark picture in the lonesome fields' to make four colour illustrations for the book, and inscribed it with what became his familiar signature, the rhythmic capitals spread out at the upper edge.

The figure subjects, which outnumber the landscapes, confirmed the talent which Jonathan Cape had been quick to spot three years earlier, when he commissioned Hilder to illustrate a shortened edition of *Moby Dick*. Those illustrations, and the ones that followed in various seafaring yarns for boys, most notably *Treasure Island*, hark back to the classic English illustrators of the 1860s. In a review of the latest crop of illustrators, *The Times* in 1929 awarded the young Hilder first place: 'He has done for the Oxford University Press a sumptuous *Treasure Island* with decorative endpapers and a number of black-and-white drawings. A certain shadowiness of conception matches ill with Stevenson's dapper precision of outline in characterisation – though Mr. Hilder's Jim Hawkins is a live and likeable boy – but the masses of dusky colour are very impressive, and the black-and-white blocks are full of power.' Of Hilder's illustrations for *Precious Bane*, the reviewer wrote: 'The energy and pathos of his line are remarkable. But we must not pass over the beauty of the coloured picture accompanying the words, "It was a fine fresh morning with a damp wind full of the scent of our ricks"; the fresh morning really shines through these leafless trees and on the blue hills.'

He has never lost his touch as a figure draughtsman; yet figures hardly ever appear in his landscapes. He senses that, however natural they may be as elements in a painting, they can be distracting, even irritating, unless they contribute directly to the 'sense' of the picture. The nearest he comes to peopling a landscape is to include a figure, perhaps a carter or a ploughman, without whose presence a particular passage in a painting might be incomplete. In street scenes, unavoidably, he adds the people and vehicles necessary to urban bustle. Even then, he treats figures less emphatically than other components, as accessories rather than participants. When his subject is pure landscape, as it almost always is these days, man's presence is felt, not seen.

Artistic talent has flourished in the Hilder family for generations. No fewer than seven of them, colaterally related, are listed as painters in Brett Hilder's monograph of his father, J.J. Hilder, one of the most renowned of early Australian landscape artists. The name has been familiar in East Sussex since Tudor times; and I have lately discovered a W. Hilder carved in the roof-beams of a 15th-century mill near Tenterden, Kent. The branch from which Rowland Hilder is descended stems from one Thomas Hilder, of Quakers Hall, Sevenoaks, a thrice-married clergyman who published a treatise on wedlock in 1653. A direct descendant, Richard Hilder, was a professional engraver; and two of his nephews, John and Richard, followed the same calling before going on to make their livings as landscape painters in the early Victorian era.

A career as a landscape painter, however, was not what Rowland Hilder had in mind when he enrolled at Goldsmiths' College, London, in 1921, at the age of sixteen. He knew he could draw, and had enough faith in his talent to look forward to an enjoyable career; but the future could take care of itself. At Goldsmiths' he was taught by E.J. Sullivan, a draughtsman and etcher of exceptional gifts whom his pupils regarded with awe. Sullivan lived in the real world, contributing illustrations to the journals and magazines. To his pupils, any man who had worked for the great magazines of the Nineties, from the *Graphic* to the *Yellow Book*, was a true professional. It was Sullivan, Hilder says, who taught him the discipline of line drawing, and with it the essential structure that holds any work of art together. Soon he began exhibiting: at the Royal Academy when he

His success as a poster artist, notably for Shell, led to such wartime commissions as this one for the Ministry of Information, on the theme 'New Life for the Land'.

was still only eighteen, and at the New English Art Club. On the two weekdays when he was not attending classes he worked in the studio of a printing firm, illustrating brochures for their customers. He left Goldsmiths' secure in his precocious talents as a draughtsman, which the College duly acknowledged by inviting him back to teach: as flattering an offer, in Hilder's view, as he has ever received.

He has never believed in the sanctity of teaching methods, or in passing on cut-and-dried values to those who come to him for advice. There are, he insists, no absolutes in art: 'It is the business of the student to find and develop a method best suited to his own temperament.' He admits that, in the past, he has been handicapped by trying to follow rules laid down by his instructors, adding: 'I have found, only after much heartache, that many of those rules, given with the best of intentions, stood in the way of the direction that I wished to go.' Himself a tireless student of earlier men's work, he finds that every rule in the book has been contradicted, and that art is as prone to fads and fashions as any other human activity. 'You only have to look at the work of contemporary artists to see that even the principles laid down by the Impressionists, whom everybody reveres, are no longer observed. The orthodoxy or innovation of one epoch can be the heresy or cliché of the next.'

His own method builds on the observation of the moment, carried later into form and structure. He seeks to record the broadest effects, working as rapidly as possible in sketch form, each one taking no more than a few minutes. Often, he may have as many as five sketches going at the same time: the sky on one can be drying while he paints the buildings or trees on another. A copse on a hill may be marked by a broad stroke of the brush, space and distance washed in by a single flowing line. A series of sketches of the same view may record the movement of cloud shadows as they pass over the landscape.

In the studio, he likes to surround himself with examples of other men's work, which he props up on his shelves or against the wall. An etching by Whistler leans against one by Ruysdael; or a colour print of a Turner finds itself in company with a dashing little study by Hercules Brabazon. His bookshelves are loaded with monographs of painters from Goya to Picasso, and illustrators from Leech to Topolski. Well-used volumes of Turner, Constable, Palmer, Sickert, Steer, sit alongside 19th-century classics of illustration such as Birket Foster's *English Land-scape* and Doré's *London*. Of his own generation he says: 'We were all young men together, so we were supposed to be "moderns" whether we liked it or not. Some liked it less than others. You felt a bit left out if, like me, you didn't know about the art "isms" of the day, or worse still thought it all rather comical.'

This was the point at which Rowland Hilder's career parted company with those of his contemporaries who, like Graham Sutherland (a fellow pupil at Goldsmiths') became dissatisfied with English ruralism and abandoned it for more adventurous modes. Hilder has never felt that compulsive tug: he is at home with his subject-matter, his deeply-felt birthright. There, too, he is on common ground with the thousands who enjoy and cherish his work, from the Christmas cards and calendars to the broad, assured and dignified landscapes of his maturity as a painter.

Taking his own road, he soon found a ready market for his work. To his obvious gifts as a draughtsman he was able to offer another: professionalism. Working to deadlines as strict as any on a national newspaper – and often in Fleet Street itself – he made a point of delivering on time, every time. To his surprise, he found certain of his book illustrations turning up, under another publisher's imprint, as greetings cards. When he complained, he was offered a contract to make more drawings of the same kind, on a royalty basis, instead of compensation. 'And that,' he will tell you, 'is how my work began appearing on people's mantelpieces …' His name also became prominent as one of the band of artists, including Graham Sutherland, John Piper, Edward Bawden, Paul Nash, who were invited by Shell to design the now-classic series of Thirties posters and advertisements encouraging the nation to take to the open road and discover the countryside. It was his work as a poster artist, celebrating parts of Britain which most families had never visited, that introduced the public at large to the distinctive Hilder style, and established his reputation among large numbers of people who spent more of their leisure time enjoying the countryside than they did in art galleries.

'Hop-picking': for a Whitbread's advertisement, 1945.

His mastery of line and tone was put severely to the test when in 1937 the Oxford University Press commissioned him to illustrate a *Bible for Today*, a version of the Testaments designed 'to offer the ordinary man an approach that he can call his own, one that is in line with his everyday knowledge and experience.' Even for the unflinching Hilder, this was a formidable task, which in the end he shared with a handful of other artists working under his supervision. It did not appear until 1941, by which time it must have seemed doubly justified. With Hilder's masterly black and white drawings, tender and powerful by turns, it became a huge bestseller. His images of towns, villages, castles, docks, with occasional landscapes suffused in an English calm, awaiting the bombs, are among the finest graphic work of his career.

The transition from graphic artist to painter came by degrees. The desire, he says, was always there; but commercial demands on his talents left him no time to be anything but a Sunday painter. A writer in *The Studio* once remarked that a visitor to his one-man exhibition at the Fine Art Gallery earlier that year would have seen little difference between the works there and what he called 'the drawings he does for a job'. But, quoting Hilder's own words, the article placed on record his desire to work more in colour, 'though I am careful not to do anything that I don't properly understand. I don't want to pick up modern tricks of style. I have just got to develop my way.' So many artists, *The Studio* added, with disciplined training behind them, had thrown it all to the winds in order to achieve something spectacular and sensational. 'Rowland Hilder's work is neither of these things. It has the sterling quality of sincerity, with a good honest purpose behind it: to draw what he sees the way he sees it, and to do it well.' The article quoted the artist's remark that, nevertheless, he was by no means averse even to surrealism: 'I like the idea. I like Dali's idea of making it rain inside a taxi with sunshine outside. It is a satisfying comment on things. The presentation of the same feeling in paint, however, is not so satisfying. I cannot overcome a certain distaste for the tedious technique that is used.'

Presentation, in the sense Hilder was speaking of, is very largely a matter of mastering techniques. No artist of his time is more skilled, or more knowledgeable, in meeting the demands of print. He knows exactly which tools are right for the job, which colours to use for reproduction purposes, how to cope with the vagaries of printers' materials. Ironically, it is this aspect of his professionalism that nudged him into the stereotype from which he has worked so hard to escape. Fifty years ago he recognised the difficulty inherent in meeting other people's demands while still remaining, as an artist, a free agent. 'People can spend their lives doing pictures in one vein. But when one is working for reproduction one has to shift

Etching has fascinated Rowland Hilder since his student days at Goldsmiths' College. Recently, his re-workings of favourite subjects in signed, limited editions have revealed him as a master of the etcher's craft.

ground very quickly. Further, a painter can make a selection of work for exhibition, but the commercial artist must exhibit prints, by the million, of a job done overnight, possibly in a fit of depression or with raging toothache!' As a public performer, an artist's reputation is always on the line.

At the outbreak of war he was among the first artists to be asked to design posters as a means of carrying a message direct to a national audience, such as 'Convoy Your Country to Victory' – merchantmen escorted across a surging sea, under the protection of the White Ensign. These posters, and the illustrated *Bible for Today*, were tasks which called upon his talents as an artist who worked for reproduction, because, as he put it at the time, 'it seemed to link up somehow with contemporary life; I have been interested in trying to put feelings into work that can be understood by most people.'

Hilder's earliest ambition was to be not a landscape painter but a marine artist. Most of his time as a young man was spent in or around boats of all kinds, sailing on the upper Thames or – somewhat later, and in a bigger craft – in the tricky waters of the Thames estuary. He delighted in the rig and tackle of ships, their intricacy and order, the way things work, the age-old skills of making and mending afloat, the messy tasks, the carpentry and cunning, seaman's lore. He has never quite lost this early infatuation. He takes off, whenever the weather looks right, for his converted coastguard's cottage at Shellness, on the eastern tip of England, where his boat is moored, either to sail, or to watch others sailing, or to paint, or all three. As a boating man himself, and a useful hand on deck, he knows how to paint marine subjects, to show vessels that sit convincingly in the water, their rig exactly trimmed for the wind and cargo. He also indulges a little nostalgia for the days when, as a young man, tall three-masters made their way up to the London docks, to moor by the Prospect of Whitby: a scene, vividly remembered, which he still returns to after sixty years.

But landscape is his true love, and his mistress. To join him on one of his painting expeditions is to share his still-boyish pleasure in setting off for a treat. We drove into a typical stretch of Hilder country on a showery day, just ahead of the spring blossom. As the by-pass turned into minor roads, and the minor roads into slushy tracks, he greeted the fields and farmland with mounting good humour. This, he said, was how he liked it, at the time of year when every shape is clear but the colours are all subdued.

Typical 'Hilderscapes' lay all around: groups of farm buildings with deep-roofed barns; a cluster of oast houses; a stack of hop-poles; a furrowed field; rain water lying in shallow, gleaming pools. He must have been to this same painting-ground a hundred times in the past fifty years; but to him it is never the same place twice. The light is always a little different. Parts of the landscape change. Or the viewpoint is one he had not noticed before. Out comes a sketchbook and pencil, and conversation stops.

He makes sketches wherever he goes, noting and recording, seeking to catch physical details, or sudden shifts in light and shade. As a landscape painter, he says, one is never satisfied. 'You long to take a bit of it away with you every time. But you know that what you are leaving behind is more important. The best you can do is settle for part of it, or for part of what it all means to you, and let your own feelings do the rest.' Painting, as a serious occupation, means bringing together everything the artist knows, or has observed, about a subject, and expressing it, he says, in an individual way. 'Some days it seems easy. You could go on and on. A week later you try again, and you can't do a thing.' His working method – recording on the spot, followed by work in the studio – is one that has been followed by generations of artists before him. He is conscious of what he owes to tradition: 'We are all followers of greater men.'

From the early 1930s, as well as his busy life as an illustrator, he was a regular exhibitor at the annual exhibitions of the Royal Institute of Painters in Water-colours. In 1964 he was elected President, an office he was to hold for the next ten years. One of his treasured possessions is an album of watercolours by members of the RI who were colleagues during his Presidency, a presentation to mark his retirement from that 150-year-old office in 1974. The RI, originally formed as a rival to the 'Old' Water Colour Society, which was founded in 1801, believed in encouraging non-professional artists as well as those who painted for a living, by opening its exhibitions to all comers. At its inaugural show there were no fewer than 120 exhibitors, rising to 170 the following year. Though the RI later modified this 'open door' policy, it has never lost sight of its original aim: its summer exhibition is still a showcase for work by professional and skilled amateur artists alike. Leading by example, Hilder has consistently supported the RI and other institutions devoted to the encouragement of watercolour.

He has been a lifelong believer in passing on his skills to others. At what was probably the most demanding time of his life, under constant pressure as an artist and illustrator, he was also lecturing to the Art Workers' Guild and giving tuition to art students at the Slade, the Royal College of Art, and the Central School of Arts and Crafts. Lately, he has been helping in a scheme to revive the fortunes of the Blackheath School of Art.

An important step towards making more time to paint was severing his connection with the Heron Press, a family business, which had been hugely successful in making him a household name. In 1963, he decided it was time to build on his second reputation as a landscape painter. The Heron operation joined forces with Royles, the printing and publishing firm, with Rowland Hilder as a director; and from that day, painting has been his life. Hitherto, his appearances at public exhibitions and in dealers' galleries had been sporadic; though it is worth remarking that, in the interval, the works he had shown in public were usually of the kind instantly recognisable as 'Hilderscapes'.

His first landscape painting to make a stir at the Royal Academy, in 1935, was something of a prototype: a winding road, elms and hayricks, crops and furrows. Hilder looks back on these early works with a fond, but not uncritical, eye. However unconsciously, they owe something to the work of such contemporaries as John and Paul Nash, and of Hilder's close friend, Douglas Percy Bliss, whose work he has helped to rescue from neglect.

During the past twenty years, with the demands of the commercial world behind him, he has been able to devote more and more time to painting. The pleasure it gives him, and the insight which deepens and enriches his work, are apparent in all he does. His landscapes show an England virtually unmarked by change. The prairie farmers have not yet ripped out the hedgerows. Carts, not tractors, stand in the sheds or rumble down the rutted tracks. No burning stubble casts its baleful glare. The soft English light falls on unpoisoned fields. We could be with Cotman, sketching along the Greta, or with Constable in the water-meadows of the Stour. Constable, in particular, is never far away in Rowland Hilder's country. It was he who insisted that an artist who fails to make the sky, the source of light, a material part of his picture, is wasting one of his greatest assets. A Hilder sky is the first element to be set down: nothing can proceed until it is right. Again, it was Constable who singled out such humdrum objects as 'old rotten banks, slimy posts, and brickwork' as the kind of scenes that made him a painter. Rowland Hilder, too, lingers on such details, at the same time absorbing them into his broad, atmospheric design.

It is significant that so many of Rowland Hilder's peers from his student days, such as Paul Drury and Robin Tanner, hold him in high regard. He recalls, without rancour, the criticism he encountered when, like them, he persisted in sticking to his chosen path. 'At that time you received no attention unless you were making news – not by getting on with your career, which I suppose is rather dull, but by dashing off in different directions looking for novelty.' At the same time, he respects most of the 'Kenneth Clark artists', as he genially calls them. 'John Nash was a particularly fine painter. You could accept his work with no difficulty, because of its underlying strength and confidence. That comes of good draughtsmanship: you have only to look at his wood engravings to see what I mean.'

Draughtsmanship, to him, has always been the key to success in painting. In a highly successful guide for beginners, *Starting with Watercolour*, he has written: 'You learn to draw by continuing to draw. Begin to draw fearlessly with something that will make a clear black line. At all costs keep going ...' He is an inveterate sketcher himself, and his eye misses nothing. I have watched him during a mid-day break, in a Shoreham pub, take a paper napkin at the bar and, so deftly as to attract no notice, sketch a pair of locals sitting barely ten feet away. Those few quick swoops of his fibre-tip pen were then folded carefully and stowed in his jacket pocket.

Instant reactions to what he sees around him find their way into his work. But in no sense is he an 'instant' painter: his method is deliberate, under full control. He uses photographs, taken himself, as well as sketchbook notes, when working out a composition. On the spot, he likes to walk right into his subject, looking at it from all angles, before settling on a conjunction of shapes and forms which, in his terms, catches the essence of the scene. If the use of a camera seems inappropriate to so gifted a painter, he points out that photography has been used by artists ever since it was invented, from Corot and Degas to Richard Hamilton and David Hockney. The mechanical image may or not bear much relation to what the artist's eye makes of the same subject; but it prompts a response in the process by which feelings and ideas, as well as direct observation, work themselves out in the act of painting.

Typically, too, he places a high value on the Englishness of English art. A staple element in such painting – from the Norwich School, Constable, Samuel Palmer and the early watercolour masters into modern times – is a close, even emotional, attachment to a place, a private sense of belonging. Rowland Hilder's landscapes now join this quietly persistent, native stream.

In the United States, where there are numerous Hilder collectors, and where part-time watercolour painting is something of a craze, Hilder's instructional books have been best-sellers. In South Africa, where he and Edith like to spend part of the winter, his work is known and admired through his appearances at the Everard Read Gallery, Johannesburg. One critic wrote: 'This master-draughtsman's art has occasionally been called old-fashioned, with no message. Yet his work pulses with love of the British countryside, and his technique is as bright, fresh and vivacious as any being done anywhere. It so happens that he is obsessed with the tranquil loveliness of the more orderly, dignified British countryside. His "message" is there in his deep involvement with centuries-old trees, buildings, bridges and country towns.' Another critic, reviewing the same exhibition in

A 1940s drawing for 'Radio Times'.

March 1981, remarked that Hilder is 'a master of all styles, yet without losing the personal vision that makes his work a coherent whole. His art personifies a stable, mature society, sure of its values. Its appeal outside such a society is partly nostalgic; but it also rests on his immense technical assurance.' The feeling of tenderness and continuity, of a countryside basking in historic calm, must seem even more poignant to exiles than it does to those nearer home.

Several painters of Hilder's stamp were commissioned by the Pilgrim Trust, at the outbreak of war, to record corners of Britain and its countryside before – it was feared – they were brutally destroyed. Their names read like a roll-call of comrades-in-arms, enlisted to help save the Old Country at a time of crisis: Thomas Hennell, Vincent Lines, Martin Hardie, Adrian Hill, Charles Knight, Stanley Badmin, Kenneth Rowntree, Rowland Suddaby. A selection of these sketches and studies was eventually published under the title *Recording Britain*. Some of the artists told of the suspicion, even hostility, they encountered from members of the public, to whom the sight of an artist with his sketchbook, with Hitler massing an army just across the Channel, was a signal to call the police. Rowland Hilder's territory was Sussex, which he shared with half-a-dozen other artists, including Sir William Russell Flint. He remembers those wartime excursions with mixed feelings: they were not particularly conducive to real painting. However, a summons by the Army, enrolling him as a Camouflage Officer, put paid to these jaunts, such as they were. Before long he was moved to the Central Office of Information, where his talents as a poster artist were put to use in keeping up morale on the Home Front. One of his posters, urging the public to support the National Savings campaign, showed a richly nostalgic expanse of farming country, accompanied by the message: 'To Enjoy the Fruits of Victory Save Now'.

For him the four decades since the war have been fruitful indeed. He has advanced his career to a point where his work is known and recognised throughout the English-speaking world. He paints what he likes, as he likes. Some of his images of England have become classics. One, 'The Garden of England', an exceptionally large watercolour which he worked on from 1945 to 1950, proved a particular favourite at the travelling exhibition 'Landscape in Britain 1850–1950', which opened at the Hayward Gallery, on London's South Bank, in 1983. For once it is not a winter scene, but spring. The trees show their first glimpses of leaf. The orchard is in blossom. The clouds ride by on an airy tide, spraying light on the oasts and barns. It is a picture suffused with affection, intelligence, and content; a Hilderscape to match them all.

DENIS THOMAS

16

TOWN AND COUNTRY

HIGH MILL, FARNHAM, SURREY

This farmstead near Farnham has many of the airs that Rowland Hilder looks for in composing a landscape, including that well-used look of a place that works for its living. Snow brings a compassionate quality to anything it touches, disguising the lie of the land so that only the bones show through, picked out in the shadows from a pale winter sun. The countryside around Farnham became familiar to Rowland Hilder during the war, when he was at the Camouflage Centre nearby.

STAITHES, NORTH YORKSHIRE

England is rich in old, well-built towns in which the bricks and stones have become part of the landscape. Places like York, Bath, King's Lynn, and the old university towns are as paintable, to a landscape artist, as the countryside around them. Rowland Hilder has drawn and painted architectural subjects all his life with hardly less pleasure than landscapes, and for many of the same reasons. It does not take much of an effort to half-close one's eyes to modern blemishes and recognise the harmonious calm which brings townscapes into the landscape painter's reckoning. Staithes is one of these: wholly without pretensions, but giving a lift to the spirit on a crisp North Yorkshire day.

DURHAM

The view of Durham from across its ancient bridge is noble enough, with its orderly masses and sturdy form. But the inside of the Cathedral is positively awesome – by general consent, the greatest Norman building in Europe. The Castle, which has been spared the usual sackings and improvements over the years, has housed Durham's University for a hundred and fifty years, and students nowadays lodge in the Keep.

CORFE CASTLE, DORSET

With its castle ruins sagging on a hill above a pretty village, mostly built from its own rubble, Corfe is one of those places that have not been the same since the Civil War. Cromwell's troops besieged the place in 1646 and wiped out most of the memorials of its past. One of these, however, may still be admired in the little museum: a dinosaur's footprint, which visitors are told is a hundred and thirty million years old.

FEBRUARY LANDSCAPE

AUTUMN AT ST JULIAN'S, SEVENOAKS

THE SWAN, LAVENHAM, SUFFOLK

THE RIVER STORT AND HARLOW MILL, ESSEX

Only part of this lovely mill still exists. Rowland Hilder made sketches of it as you see it here some fifty years ago, while on his way to Cambridge. Most of the structure was later destroyed by fire.

WHICHFORD, WARWICKSHIRE

WINTER ANGLERS

POND BY 'THE PRINCE OF WALES', BLACKHEATH

Blackheath has been the Hilder family home, with only a few interruptions, for fifty years: they moved across the Heath from Lee Park to Kidbrooke Grove in 1935. As well as the much-travelled car, there is often a boat parked behind the front hedge. Rowland Hilder enjoys Blackheath: the shops, the architecture, the walks, and above all, perhaps, the brilliant light and dramatic skies, unusual in such an urban location. Today, the Heath is a huge natural playing field, where at weekends the scene flickers with the colours of a hundred football shirts.

ROWLAND HILL

29

FAVERSHAM, KENT

Faversham is connected to the River Swale by Faversham Creek, and it is possible to come ashore there to enjoy a ramble among its tidy houses and trim little shops. It was once nearly blown to pieces when a gunpowder store exploded, but the gaps seem to have been filled in with sensible good taste. It is one of those pleasing little towns which, once discovered, it is as well to keep to oneself.

CHARLECOTE, WARWICKSHIRE

As every schoolboy knows, or used to, Charlecote Park was where Shakespeare was caught poaching deer, duly punished, and in revenge wrote a scurrilous lampoon on the landowner, Sir Thomas Lucy, which set him on his way to London determined to seek his fortune as a writer. The house was built in 1558. Like many an English architectural masterpiece, it now belongs to the National Trust.

SMITH'S FARM, ALLHALLOWS, ISLE OF GRAIN

BARN INTERIOR, ALLHALLOWS

Rowland Hilder makes a practice of walking into a landscape and its buildings, getting the feel of them, noting their relationship to one another. From time to time an interior suggests itself as a separate theme. A line and wash drawing done on the spot helps to catch the airiness and dignity of the subject.

BAINBRIDGE, NORTH YORKSHIRE

LYMINGTON, HAMPSHIRE

Lymington is a haven for yachtsmen which also happens to have an older quarter, where one is reminded that this must be the historic starting point for the Isle of Wight, just across the water. The breezy bustle of these seaside places offers endless subjects for an artist's sketchbook. A rough pen sketch of this subject is on page 117.

THE MERE

Mood, to Rowland Hilder, is as personal as a feeling for location. Some compositions, such as this one, are based largely on reconstruction and recall.

TUG AND LIGHTERS, CAMBRIDGESHIRE

LINCOLN

Lincoln is associated with another of Rowland Hilder's heroes among water-colour painters, Peter De Wint, who as the son of a Dutchman seemed very much at home in the calm flat landscape of the Fens. Seeing a subject through another painter's eyes is inevitable if, like Hilder, you have studied your predecessors with professional admiration. He shares De Wint's preference for a limited palette – but is thankful that modern pigments are more durable.

CLEY MILL, NORFOLK

Norfolk has a more rugged landscape than Suffolk, nowhere more invigoratingly so than along its north coast, where winds race across sand-dunes and marshes and flint-built houses huddle in comfortable groups. On the map it says Cley-next-the-Sea, but that was before a slice of land was reclaimed three hundred years ago. In Norfolk, 'Cley' is pronounced 'Cly'.

DECEMBER SNOW

BOSTON STUMP AND MARKET SQUARE, LINCOLNSHIRE

The famous Boston 'Stump' is the octagonal tower of St Botolph's Church, looming above the River Witham just inshore from Freiston. Boston has gone downhill, like its neighbour across the water, King's Lynn, since the Wash began to silt up. The Stump still acts as a marker for ships out in the Wash. Bostonians from New England looking for their ancestors are impressed.

KING'S LYNN, NORFOLK

To arrive at King's Lynn by sea is a more dramatic landfall than simply coming to the end of a long flat road. The architecture has that well-bred English air about it: King John gave the town its character in the twelfth century, and it has worn well. The Customs House, which dominates this quayside subject, dates from the seventeenth century. Things have not been the same at Lynn, as the locals call it, since the maritime traffic dried up. But there is a salty air to the place, fresh off the Wash, and people come a long way to enjoy its arts festival in the summer.

NORWICH CATHEDRAL

Norwich's Cathedral is as splendid as a city so full of art deserves. The Norwich artists knew it as part of their native townscape. Some of them went to the Free School there, in the Cathedral Close, and a couple of them gave art lessons there to the boys. John Sell Cotman set up as a drawing master in a handsome house on St Martin's Plain, just over the wall. A favourite viewpoint is Pull's Ferry, much painted and photographed, seen from across the narrow river on the Thorpe side, where stones to build the Cathedral were brought in by water right up to the site before the access was filled in.

THE THAMES FROM SHELL-MEX HOUSE

FLATFORD BRIDGE, NEAR DEDHAM, SUFFOLK

Like generations of English painters, Rowland Hilder has responded to Suffolk and Norfolk, where the landscape seems permeated with the imagery of Gainsborough, John Crome, John Sell Cotman and Constable. The short stretch of the Stour which provided Constable with so many of his best-loved subjects is still more or less intact. Flatford Bridge is the modern successor to the cattle bridge which Constable stood on to make sketches for his 'Flatford Mill' in 1817. Within a few hundred yards were familiar scenes and themes. 'The sound of water escaping from milldams,' he said, 'willows, old rotten planks, slimy posts and brickwork – I love such things.'

THE GARDEN OF ENGLAND

Rowland Hilder is sometimes asked why he prefers to paint the English countryside in its winter garb rather than in its full leafy beauty. As it happens, the painting which has most often been shown in public exhibitions as a typical example of his work, 'The Garden of England', shows the Kentish landscape at the burgeoning of Spring. The artist has never parted with it, and its location remains his secret.

UPPER SLAUGHTER, COTSWOLDS

FOUR STUDIES OF ENGLISH WILD FLOWERS,
IN COLLABORATION WITH EDITH HILDER

APRIL

JULY

AUGUST

NOVEMBER

THE BACKS, CAMBRIDGE

Few places in Europe can rival the view across the Cam to King's College Chapel, Clare College, Trinity and St John's, with the greensward sweeping down to the river bank. In summer, people like to sit along the edge watching punters navigate this blissful but muddy-bottomed stretch. Novices, and elders who only half-remember how to do it, are apt to fall in to loud applause.

WINTER LANDSCAPE

THE DEVIL'S BRIDGE, KIRKBY LONSDALE, CUMBRIA

CANTERBURY, KENT

A writer on Canterbury, a city that still stands as a pillar of Christendom, once described it as bearing 'the lovely features of a resigned age'. To secure this viewpoint, Rowland Hilder had to find his way on to the roof of a nearby cinema.

SPRING IN THE DALES

WINTER PLOUGHING

Here is a scene that has lost much of its hold on our affections since tractors took over from horses. Turning over the earth, fertilising and sowing, are routines that men in all ages and all countries have celebrated with rituals and magic-making. The ploughman's pride was to cut a dead straight furrow, turn, then cut another, and another, till the task was done. Nothing reveals the shape of the land more movingly, in Rowland Hilder's eyes, than these rugged parallel lines, drawn or dragged over its surface with a deep-cutting blade. It was one of the first country scenes to excite him as a young painter, and it excites him still.

HAMBLEDEN MILL

Here, by a lock on the Thames north-east of Henley, the handsome water-mill, clad in white weatherboards, looms above the reeds and passing pleasure-craft. Below this peaceful spot, just beyond the weir, the water is rough enough to challenge the skill of canoeists. Below: a publicity drawing of Ightham Mote, near Sevenoaks, from the 1930s.

POLPERRO, CORNWALL

People tend to have a soft spot for this former smuggling village, the only one to have set up a Museum of Smuggling in honour of its shady past. The mainstay of the villagers, however, has been fishing; though these days the fishermen bob about offshore with summer holiday-makers trying to catch the local mackerel, which usually oblige.

ROWLAND HILDER

THE IRON BRIDGE AT COALBROOKDALE, SHROPSHIRE

SEA AND SHORE

SAILING BOATS BECALMED

Nowhere, in Rowland Hilder's favourite painting country, is he very far from water. Boating on the rivers of Kent has been one of his pleasures, though surpassed, for incident and excitement, by bracing adventures under sail in the open sea. A marine artist is what he started out to be, and his feeling for the mariner's way of life has never left him.

ROWLAND HILDER —

THE SWALE AT QUEENBOROUGH, ISLE OF SHEPPEY

Low tide brings together features which Rowland Hilder enjoys best in marine subjects: soft light, the glint of sun on water, and a surrounding landscape showing through. At such times, subject and composition fall naturally into place. Any boating man knows the pleasurable sounds that accompany such scenes, the cry of sea birds, the rattling of the rigging, the lazy slurp of the water. The salty flats at Shellness, at the edge of the open sea, can always be depended on to send Rowland Hilder home with something worthy of those moments when earth, sea and sky seem suspended in thin air.

The Isle of Sheppey, the extreme eastward tip of Kent, is where Rowland Hilder rents a converted coastguard's cottage, his base for sailing the tricky waters of the Swale. The light there is remarkable, and the skies can be huge. Many of the marine subjects he has painted and exhibited with the Royal Society of Marine Artists are of these waters on the very edge of England.

DISTANT ESTUARY

The Dutch and English traditions in marine painting are both evident in Rowland Hilder's treatment of the theme: big skies, low horizons, and the relationship between sea and moisture-laden air.

THE MILLSTREAM

BEACHED BOATS, HASTINGS, EAST SUSSEX

Hastings, known to the world as the place where the Normans landed in 1066 (though historically that was Pevensey Bay, just down the coast), is familiar to painters for its picturesque beach, on which stand tall wooden huts where the local fishermen store their gear, as they have since Elizabethan times. It was an original member of the Cinque Ports; and it is still possible to buy fish straight off the boat as the fishermen return with their catch. There is hardly a marine artist of any importance who did not, at some time, paint the scene. Says Rowland Hilder: 'I also love to study the age-old structure of these sturdy little craft, built to be buffeted by the waves. Even when they are hauled up the shingle they look trim, tight, and ready for action.'

THE ESTUARY

TEWKESBURY MILL

OLD TIDAL MILL, BIRDHAM, WEST SUSSEX

This subject appeals to Rowland Hilder for its combination of elements – sky, water, buildings, boats, a glimpse of landscape – and for its antiquity. Birdham, on the estuary near Chichester, is among the last surviving tidal mills in the country.

THE CREEK, EARLY MORNING

GREENWICH YACHT CLUB, BUGSBY'S REACH

YACHT CLUB AT THE CREEK, STORM APPROACHING

TOP LOCK, STOKE BRUERNE, NORTHAMPTONSHIRE

Here, on the Grand Canal, an old ware-house by the lock has been turned into a museum marking the great age of the 'narrow boats', when the canals were the arteries of the industrial network. There is a hint of those times in the surviving buildings; and painted barges, now used as pleasure craft, bring touches of colour to a very different scene.

TOWER BRIDGE

THE THAMES AT WAPPING

ROWLAND HILDER

THE PROSPECT OF WHITBY, WAPPING WALL

While he was still in his teens, Rowland Hilder likes to recall, he used to venture along the Thames in a tiny sailing dingy, fascinated by the sailing barges and by the activity of the dockside, where men clambered or crouched amid a forest of masts and spars. Gradually he learned to work out what they were doing, the age-old crafts of the boatmen and riggers, the mysteries of seamanship as recounted in boys' adventure stories. His first ambition was to be a marine painter. The details he stored away, the sights and sounds of the busy river, have remained vivid ever since. When he thinks of the Thames, that once-noble river, he thinks of it as he knew it then – alive, urgent, mysterious, and with waterside pubs whose names have become legendary. 'For as long as I paint the Thames,' he says, 'that is how it will be.'

OLD THAMES-SIDE, GREENWICH

For an artist who made some of his first drawings and sketches along its banks, the Thames retains its lifelong hold on the imagination, however much the scene may change.

SALTINGS ON THE BLACKWATER

THE ESTUARY, LOW TIDE

CORNERS IN KENT

OASTS IN SPRING

The white-capped kilns which catch the eye in the Weald of Kent – commonly called 'oasts', though that is strictly the name for the whole building – are as native to the Weald as oysters are to Whitstable. They are not decorations, but essential aids to the process by which hops are dried before they go off to the brewers – a process that involves draughts and fires, carefully regulated so as not to singe or scorch the crop spread on the drying floor. Over the years, more and more of these desirable places have been turned into private homes. But they still need their white caps: a kiln without its bonnet, any painter would agree, looks undressed. This composition is based on a group of oast-houses near Chiddingstone, as on page 109.

85

SHOREHAM VALLEY

Rowland Hilder never tires of this, his first love as a landscape painter: the peaceful valley that moved Samuel Palmer to his images of an earthly paradise when he lived there over 150 years ago. Says Rowland Hilder: 'Some fellow students and I discovered Palmer together when we were at Goldsmiths' College, so I went out to find Shoreham for myself, taking a camera with me. I photographed the farms and oasts, and walked the lanes. I discovered that one of my photographs was of Sepham Barn, one of Palmer's subjects. It had not changed in a hundred years. Later, when I went back, it had been knocked down and a new tin one was there in its place. I can't bring myself to include that modern version in my paintings of Shoreham.'

EARLY MORNING SHADOWS

MUCK-SPREADING NEAR SHOREHAM

Muck-spreading does not sound like a painterly subject, perhaps. But to Rowland Hilder it typifies an aspect of the English agricultural scene which chastens many a city-dweller – the unremitting hunger of the soil. It is this side of the farmer's life which the Instamatic view cannot reveal, much less explain. 'Painters have taught us how to enjoy the picturesque,' Rowland Hilder says. 'But I like to think there is something of value in nature which has nothing to do with prettiness alone.'

ROWLAND HILDER

THE LANE, HIGH HALSTOW

It is difficult to find on the map, and it is nowhere in particular for anyone looking for a day out. But High Halstow, or rather this rather nondescript part of it, has been, for Rowland Hilder, a source of studies and drawings for over fifty years. A young man who had been an art student with him at Goldsmiths', Norman Hepple,

joined him in renting an old disused pub there, for a sketching holiday. From the front windows was this view of the neighbouring farm, which stood on a lane that led to a bird sanctuary. 'We were invited by a keen bird–watcher to join him in one of the hides, to watch a nest of baby herons. I disgraced myself by

making an accidental noise, whereupon all the babies were simultaneously sick. When my mother, a true countrywoman, saw my drawing of the farm, she asked why I should want to do a picture showing people's outside privy. I am still using this subject. A few months ago I turned it into one of my larger etchings.'

FARM NEAR LAMBERHURST

CHILHAM

An old church, a market square, a comfort-able inn, groups of ancient houses and shop-fronts, all make Chilham one of the most paintable of English villages. The Kentish Stour trickles at the foot of the neighbouring hill.

A COUNTRY LANE NEAR COWDEN

THE OLD FORD AND BRIDGE, EYNSFORD

This is another spot in the Shoreham Valley that has hardly changed. The bridge manages to deal with the traffic on busy weekends, when people come to enjoy the scenery, the pub, the ruins of the local castle, or the walk along the Darent at Lullingstone, with its reconstituted Roman villa, its Queen Anne mansion and tiny church set in a swathe of green. From here you can still walk through relatively unspoiled countryside all the way to Otford. A watercolour sketch of this subject is on page 123.

KNOLE HOUSE AND PARK, SEVENOAKS

Knole is one of the great houses of Kent, and of England, a princely establishment that passed from royal hands (those of Henry VIII, who filched it from Archbishop Cranmer) to those of the Sackville family, and thence into the care of the National Trust. Its ancient courts, halls, furnishings and treasures, and the ageless grounds of the huge deer park, have hardly changed in four hundred years. A landscape painter looking around him here is aware that he is by no means the first to pull out his sketchbook. The view of the front of the house, with the inevitable posing deer, was painted by Paul Sandby in the 1770s very much as you see it here.

THE WEALD

The Weald occupies by far the greater part of the county of Kent. The Pilgrims Way, running along the North Downs, offers superb views of it. The Shoreham Valley, north of Sevenoaks, runs into it. The new motorways, which have brought some scenic benefits as well as losses, have opened up unexpected views across this wide expanse, all of which was dense forest from Anglo-Saxon times until centuries of clearances made it habitable. Now, it is the heart of the Garden of England, rich in villages and small farms, a total environment. Rowland Hilder has known it all his life, and once lived, with his young family, in an old house that commanded these extensive views. It has remained his favourite painting ground.

THE INNER HARBOUR, QUEENBOROUGH, ISLE OF SHEPPEY

ROWLAND HILDER

ST CLEMENT'S CHURCH, OLD ROMNEY

St Clement's Church, Old Romney, sits in its own fields with a great yew tree for company. It has been there for seven hundred years, and inside it is almost untouched Georgian. Outside, the famous Romney sheep chomp the lush Romney grass. This is like nowhere else in Kent, with its uncannily clear light, its feeling of space, and the presence of the sea always just over the next field. Dr Parry, Bishop of Dover, described it in an address to the Kent Archaeological Society a hundred years ago. 'Where are we? Is this Kent? Are we in England at all, or have we dropped down somewhere on the Campagna, outside the walls of Rome?' Fairfield Church, dedicated to St Thomas of Canterbury, stands by itself in a huge wet empty landscape, alongside a dyke. It was rescued from complete ruin early this century, and you can reach it by a footpath in dry weather. People come to Romney Marsh just to 'collect' the churches. There are some twenty of them, all bearing charmed lives in this spellbound landscape.

FAIRFIELD CHURCH, ROMNEY MARSH

THE TITHE BARN

FARM NEAR SHOREHAM

AYLESFORD

The Medway between Maidstone and Tonbridge runs through some of the most delightful scenery in Kent. It looks its best from a boat, as views unfold round bends and under bridges. There are five such bridges: at Aylesford, East Farleigh, Teston (pronounced Teeson), and two at Yalding. The bridge at East Farleigh, as you pass under it, is ribbed like a church roof. General Fairfax marched his men over it to attack Maidstone in the Civil War; otherwise it has had a quiet life.

TESTON BRIDGE

OASTHOUSES, CHIDDINGSTONE

WINTER BEFORE SNOW

ROWLAND HILDER

A GRAVESEND SHRIMPER

LIGHTS AND SHADES

John Crome, the 'father' of the Norwich School of painters, spoke of composition forming 'one grand plan of light and shade,' adding: 'Trifles in Nature must be over looked, that we may have our spirits raised by seeing the whole picture at a glance.' Rowland Hilder has followed these principles, not only in his most painterly work but also in his black-and-white landscape studies and in his etchings. He came to watercolour through the use of line and wash, which seemed to offer the best way of making use of his ability to draw. A favourite method of his own, he tells students, is to draw with a piece of sharpened stick dipped in Indian ink. 'The wood absorbs a certain amount of ink and acts as a natural reservoir. It makes a brisk, rough, granulated line when used on rough paper.' Form and structure, he maintains, are achieved by counterchange – dark shapes against light, light against dark, which he perceives as a basic principle of nature as well as of art. Turner, he points out, once overcame the formality of the two domes of the Royal Naval College, Greenwich, by showing one in strong sunlight and the other as a dark silhouette, overcast by the shadow of a passing cloud.

THROUGH THE SUNLIGHT
WINDOW

THE THAMES AND ST PAUL'S

The title to this double-page illustration, for *The Bible for Today*, reads: 'Until Every City of the World has Become a City of God'. Rowland Hilder, sharing the task of illustrating the work with a small team of like-minded artists, was responsible for the most important contributions. This task, the editor wrote in his preface, demanded from the artist 'a mind sensitive to the modern spirit, and able to enter with sympathetic understanding into the Editor's purpose.'

'The good draughtsman,' says Rowland Hilder in his advice to students, 'keeps the drawing alive. He does not overload the work, making it static and tedious: he keeps to essentials, making a crisp, clear statement.' These examples from his own sketchbooks show how he records essential information in a quick first glance, adding a word here and there on particular points of colour emphasis or light, suggesting forms as well as outlines, and working towards a combination of line and tone shorthand technique, as he calls it, 'making a statement that will become the basis of a good watercolour style.'

This rapid sketch of a corner of Lymington, Hampshire, was the starting-point for
the watercolour reproduced on page 35.

If a drawing is going well, Rowland Hilder says, 'you begin to sense the rhythmic effect of certain kinds of line arrangements, and to appreciate that a complicated piece of work will be seen better when it is placed against a simple background. The art of drawing, as of painting, is that of selection and simplification.'

Trees, in Rowland Hilder's experience, are both impossibly complicated to draw and satisfyingly simple once the various parts are seen as a whole. To him, a sketch of a tree can be as complete, in its way, as a study that might have taken hours. 'You should ask yourself whether you wish to make a portrait of a particular tree or whether it is to be a factor in the general landscape. If the latter, it should be painted simply and clearly as a pattern of tone and colour. If this is done successfully it will look convincing, even if it is only indicated by a few bold strokes of the brush.'

THE TRACK TO THE FARM

AYLESFORD BRIDGE

Watercolours left in an 'unfinished' state, as on these two pages, make their own direct impression. The interior is Rowland Hilder's painting room in his cottage at Shellness. The bridge opposite is the familiar viewpoint at Eynesford, of which another version is on page 97.

123

Printmaking now occupies much of Rowland Hilder's inventiveness and energy. This etching of the lane near High Halstow, Kent, is a variant, in reverse, of a favourite subject: a watercolour version is on page 92. The landscape on page 126 is a combination of etching and aquatint. The little 'Hilderscape' of farm buildings on page 127 is a softground etching, a technique brought to its highest point early in the last century by John Sell Cotman.

Bibliography

BOOKS BY ROWLAND HILDER

Starting with Watercolour Studio Vista 1966

Painting Landscapes in Watercolour Collins 1983

BOOKS ILLUSTRATED BY ROWLAND HILDER

The Riddle of the Air Percy F. Westerman, Blackie 1925

Moby Dick Herman Melville, Jonathan Cape 1926

The Adventures of a Trafalgar Lad John Lesterman, Jonathan Cape 1926

The Junior Cadet Percy F. Westerman, Blackie 1927

A Sailor of Napoleon John Lesterman, Jonathan Cape 1927

A Pair of Rovers John Lesterman, Jonathan Cape 1928

The Second Mate of the Myradale John Lesterman, Jonathan Cape 1929

Treasure Island Robert Louis Stevenson 1929

Then and Now Shell Mex Ltd 1929

Precious Bane Mary Webb, Jonathan Cape 1929

Kidnapped Robert Louis Stevenson, Oxford University Press 1930

The Senior Cadet Percy F. Westerman, Blackie 1931

Little Peter the Great H.A. Manhood, Jackson 1931

The Midnight Folk John Masefield, Heinemann 1931

Three Tales of the Sea C. Fox-Smith, Oxford University Press 1932

In Defence of British Rivers, Shell Mex and BP Ltd 1932

Fire Down Below W.M.W. Watt, Muller 1935

They Went to the Island L.A.G. Strong, Dent 1940

In collaboration: *The Bible for Today*, Oxford University Press 1941

In collaboration with Edith Hilder: *The Shell Guide to Flowers of the Countryside* Geoffrey Grigson, Phoenix House 1955

Index of subjects and places